Deliciously Low

by Harriet Roth

with a Foreword by John W. Farquhar, M.D.

HARRIET ROTH has a B.S. in nutrition from Carnegie Mellon
University. A former student of Simone Beck and Roger Verget,
she taught French and Italian cookery for 18 years, until her
appointment as Director of the Pritikin Longevity Center
Cooking School.